WHY I LOVE YOU

Romantic gift journal
for Valentine's day / anniversary

BARCELOVER

To: _ _ _ _ _ _ _ _ _ _ _ _ _ _

With love

From: _ _ _ _ _ _ _ _ _ _ _ _

This book is a tool to let you know why I love you.

(and how much!)

I love you because...

My first impression of you was

Your kisses taste like...

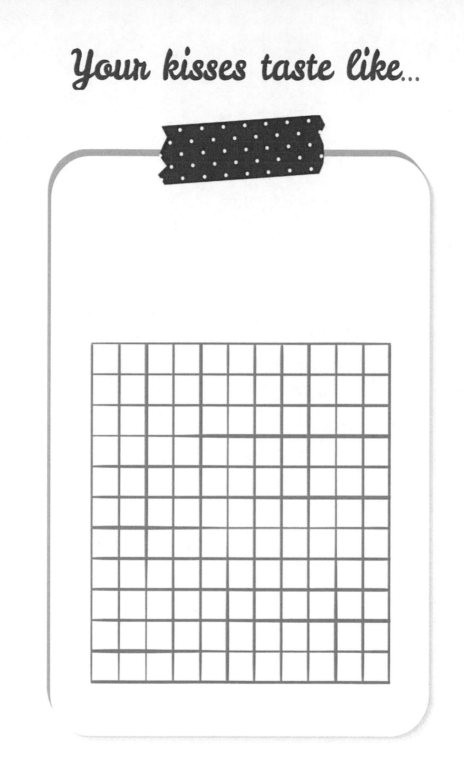

I knew you were the one when...

The 4 things that have improved my life since we met, are...

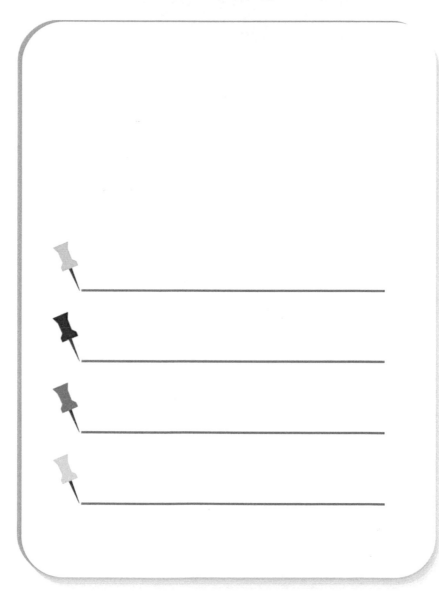

The best advice you have ever given me is...

Something I know about you
that the rest of the world
doesn´t

TOP SECRET

You bring out the best in me, specifically by. . .

Our most
romantic moments are:

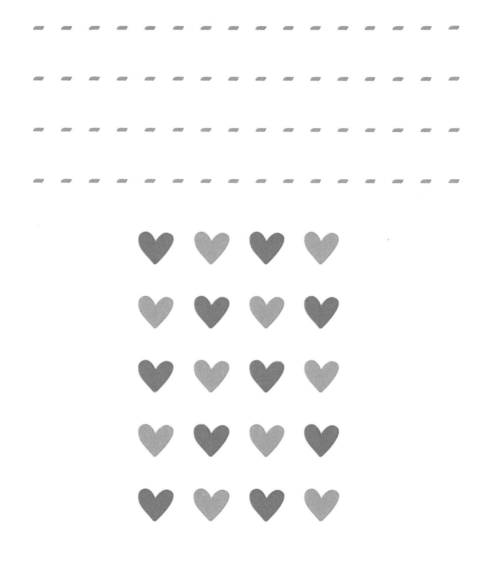

My favorite picture of us is this one (paste here)

What is unique in our relationship is

The significant milestone in our relationship is

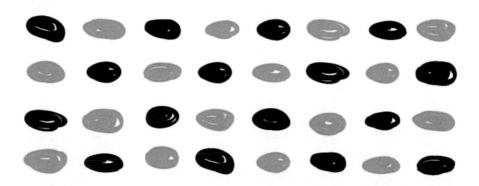

I first knew I loved you when

- -

- -

- -

- -

- -

- -

I LOVE DOING

THESE THINGS

WITH YOU

- - - - - - - - - - - - - - - - -

- - - - - - - - - - - - - - - - -

- - - - - - - - - - - - - - - - -

- - - - - - - - - - - - - - - - -

- - - - - - - - - - - - - - - - -

What I wanted to tell you, but I never had the time before is

The way I usually express how much I love is

- -

- -

- -

- -

LOVE COUPONS

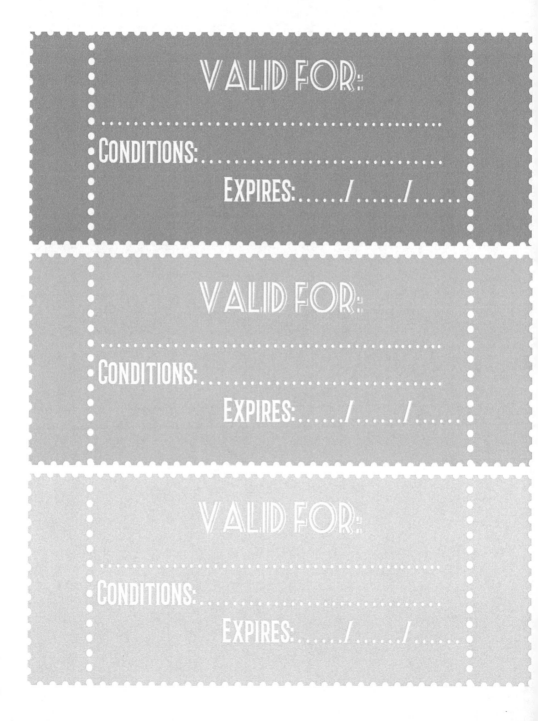

VALID FOR:

....

Conditions:..

Expires:......./......./......

VALID FOR:

....

Conditions:..

Expires:......./......./......

VALID FOR:

....

Conditions:..

Expires:......./......./......

What I miss from you when you are not around is

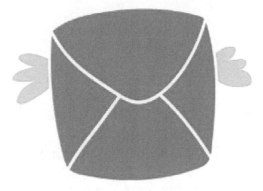

- -
- -
- -
- -
- -
- -

29000721R00024

Made in the USA
Middletown, DE
03 February 2016